nature's
baby animals

BABY ANIMALS
OF THE OCEAN

Carmen Bredeson

Dennis L. Claussen, Ph.D., *Series Science Consultant* Professor of Zoology, Miami University, Oxford, Ohio

Allan A. De Fina, Ph.D., *Series Literacy Consultant* Past President of the New Jersey Reading Association, Chairperson, Department of Literacy Education, New Jersey City University, Jersey City, New Jersey

CONTENTS

ENDANGERED ANIMAL OF THE OCEAN

WORDS TO KNOW

anemone (uh NEH muh nee)—A soft sea animal that looks like a flower.

blubber (BLUH bur)—A layer of fat under the skin.

endangered (en DAYN jurd) **animal**— A type of animal that may disappear from Earth forever.

poisonous (POY zun us)— Something that can hurt or kill people and animals.

pouch (powch)—A bag used to hold something.

WHERE ARE OCEANS?

3

THE OCEAN

Oceans cover much of the Earth. Some oceans are warm and some oceans are cold. All oceans have salt water.

The ocean is home to many kinds of animals. Baby animals have special ways to stay safe and live in the ocean.

warm ocean

cold ocean

BABY **HARP SEAL**

Harp seal pups are born on the ice. Their fur is as white as snow. The pups learn to swim when they are only a few weeks old. Their thick fur and **blubber** keep them warm in the very cold water.

Baby dolphins make many sounds. They click, whistle, and squeak. That is how they talk to their mothers. Dolphins swim in groups. Swimming together is safer than swimming alone.

BABY
BOTTLENOSE DOLPHIN

BABY SEA OTTER

A sea otter pup rides on its mother's belly. She teaches her pup to swim and look for food. Sea otters find snails and crabs to eat. They use rocks to crack open the shells. Sea otters float on their backs while eating.

This baby turtle has a lot of growing to do!

Sea turtles lay eggs in the sand. The eggs hatch and the babies crawl to the ocean. They hide in seaweed and eat small crabs and shrimp.

BABY
SEA TURTLE

A little hermit crab finds a new home.

BABY
HERMIT CRAB

eggs

A hermit crab begins life in the ocean. It hatches from an egg and looks like a little fish. Soon it turns into a tiny crab and crawls onto the shore. The crab moves into a little seashell. As the crab grows, it moves to bigger and bigger shells.

anemone

eggs

The mother clown fish lays eggs under sea **anemones**. After the eggs hatch, the babies stay near the **poisonous** anemones. The anemone's sting does not hurt the clown fish. Other animals stay away from the anemone. The baby clown fish are safe.

Clown fish are also called anemonefish.

BABY
CLOWN FISH

BABY **SEAHORSE**

Baby seahorses grow inside eggs. Their father carries the eggs in a **pouch** on his belly. After the babies hatch, their father squirts them into the water. The babies hide in seaweed from hungry fish and crabs.

A father seahorse and his new babies.

Blue whales are the biggest animals on Earth. A blue whale pup is as long as a school bus when it is born. It stays close to its huge mother. There are not many blue whales left. They have been hunted for their blubber and for their meat.

ENDANGERED
ANIMAL OF
THE OCEAN

BABY
BLUE WHALE

Books

Bingham, Caroline. *Whales and Dolphins.*
New York: DK Publishing, 2003.

Rose, Deborah Lee. *Ocean Babies.* Washington, D.C.:
National Geographic Children's Books, 2005.

Simon, Seymour. *Oceans.* New York: Harper Collins,
2006.

Stille, Darlene R. *I Am a Fish: The Life of a Clown Fish.* Minneapolis, Minn.: Picture Window Books, 2005.

National Geographic Kids
http://kids.nationalgeographic.com/animals/fish.html

Planet Ocean
http://school.discovery.com/schooladventures/
     planetocean/

INDEX

~To our little Texans~Andrew, Charlie, and Kate~

Enslow Elementary, an imprint of Enslow Publishers, Inc.
Enslow Elementary® is a registered trademark of Enslow Publishers, Inc.

Copyright © 2009 by Carmen Bredeson

Library of Congress Cataloging-in-Publication Data

Bredeson, Carmen.
    Baby animals of the ocean / Carmen Bredeson.
        p. cm. — (Nature's baby animals)
    Summary: "Up-close photos and information about baby animals of the ocean biome"—Provided by publisher.
    Includes bibliographical references and index.
    ISBN-13: 978-0-7660-3003-9
    ISBN-10: 0-7660-3003-2
    1. Marine animals—Infancy—Juvenile literature. I. Title.
QL122.2.B74 2009
591.77—dc22
                            2007039469

Printed in the United States of America

10 9 8 7 6 5 4 3 2 1

Note to Parents and Teachers: The **Nature's Baby Animals** series supports the National Science Education Standards for K–4 science. The Words to Know section introduces subject-specific vocabulary words, including pronunciation and definitions. Early readers may need help with these new words.

To Our Readers: We have done our best to make sure all Internet addresses in this book were active and appropriate when we went to press. However, the author and the publisher have no control over and assume no liability for the material available on those Internet sites or on other Web sites they may link to. Any comments or suggestions can be sent by e-mail to comments@enslow.com or to the address on the back cover.

Every effort has been made to locate all copyright holders of material used in this book. If any errors or omissions have occurred, corrections will be made in future editions of this book.

Photo Credits: © 1999, Artville, LLC, p. 3; © 2008 Judy Holmes/AlaskaStock.com, pp. 6, 23; © Bill Wood/NHPA/Photoshot, p. 15; © Charlie Phillips/SplashdownDirect, pp. 2 (left), 9; © Darryl Bush/drr.net, p. 8; David Hall/Photo Researchers, Inc., p. 16; © Francois Gohier/ardea.com, p. 21; © George Grall/Getty Images, p. 18; Minden Pictures: © Chris Newbert, pp. 2 (right), 17, © Frans Lanting, p. 11, © Michio Hoshino, p. 7; © Nathan Cohen/Visuals Unlimited, p. 12; naturepl.com: © Doug Perrine, pp. 13, 19, © Jane Burton, p. 14; © Phillip Colla/Oceanlight.com, p. 20; Shutterstock, p. 5; © Tom & Pat Leeson/ardea.com, pp. 1, 10.

Cover Photo: © Tom & Pat Leeson/ardea.com

Enslow Elementary
an imprint of
Enslow Publishers, Inc.

40 Industrial Road
Box 398
Berkeley Heights, NJ 07922
USA
http://www.enslow.com